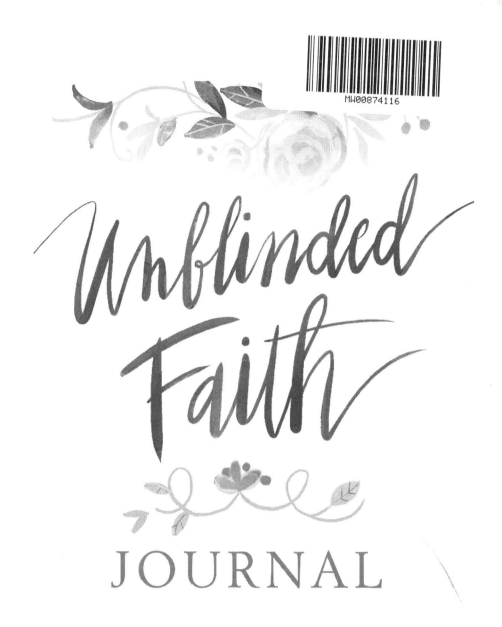

Unblinded Faith

JOURNAL

UNBLINDEDFAITH.COM

May the glorious light of the Good News
shine bright in you and through you
all the days of your life.

Inspired by
2 Corinthians 4:4 NLT

A Journey of Prayer

Have you heard that the process of physically writing down your thoughts using pen and paper is incredibly beneficial for the retention and reflection process?

I've found it to be especially true in my life, especially since I'm a kinesthetic learner. You'll find me with a journal in hand and scribbling out notes any time I have to listen to a sermon. The same is true when it comes to reading Scripture. I use a pencil for underlining in my Bible and a gel highlighter for bringing emphasis to the principles I believe God wants me to pay close attention too. My journal is also open and poised for writing down verses I want to memorize as well as for scribbling down my prayers. It's amazing how this process invites me deeper into the Word and provides a legacy of faith-in-progress to build upon. That's what I want for you.

It is my deepest hope and prayer that you'll do more than just read the words I've shared in Unblinded Faith, but that you'll respond personally to God's Truth.

I hope you'll open your copy of UNBLINDED FAITH, along with your Bible and this journal, to begin the kind of life-changing, legacy building-ing relationship with God I've experienced with God. You may choose to use the space provided to:

- re-write the key Scripture verse
- turn the key Scripture verse into a prayer
- reflect upon the key question
- talk with God about how to apply the Word of God to your life

However you choose to move through this journey of gaining spiritual sight, I pray that it results in a deeper, more abiding confidence in the Word of God and in our Savior, Jesus Christ.

Becoming More Like Jesus with You,

Elisa Pulliam

"…the deepest spiritual lessons are not learned
by his letting us have our way in the end,
but by his making us wait,
bearing with us in love and patience
until we are able to honestly pray
what he taught his disciples to pray:
Thy will be done."

Elizabeth Elliot

Made to See

Satan, who is the god of this world, has blinded the minds of those who don't believe. They are unable to see the glorious light of the Good News. They don't understand this message about the glory of Christ, who is the exact likeness of God. 2 CORINTHIANS 4:4 NLT

_____

_____

_____

_____

_____

_____

_____

_____

_____

_____

_____

_____

_____

_____

_____

_____

_____

_____

_____

_____

_____

We need to cultivate unblinded faith,
which comes by believing God's Word is true.

1. Prepared & Equipped

All Scripture is inspired by God and is useful to teach us what is true and to make us realize what is wrong in our lives. It corrects us when we are wrong and teaches us to do what is right. God uses it to prepare and equip his people to do every good work. 2 TIMOTHY 3:16-17 NLT

_____

_____

_____

_____

_____

_____

_____

_____

_____

_____

_____

_____

_____

_____

_____

_____

*If we long to face each day prepared
and equipped, we need to start each
day inspired and steeped in the Word.*

2. You Know Everything

You observe my wanderings and my sleeping, my waking and my dreaming, and You know everything I do in more detail than even I know. PSALM 139:3 NLT

He made us. He watches us.
He knows us better than anyone
else in this world.

3. Something New

I am about to do something new. See, I have already begun! Do you not see it? I will make a pathway through the
wilderness. I will create rivers in the dry wasteland. ISAIAH
43:19 NLT

A life without risk forsakes the
opportunities for our faith to grow.

4. Take Heart

I have told you these things, so that in me you may have
peace. In this world you will have trouble. But take heart! I
have overcome the world. JOHN 16:33 NLT

Heaven is the final trouble-free destination
for the beloved of God!

5. He Will Continue

I am certain that God, who began the good work within you, will continue his work until it is finally finished on the day when Christ Jesus returns. PHILIPPIANS 1:6 NLT

Sometimes what appears to be the end of
the story is simply the end of a chapter.

6. Filled Souls

Father, out of Your honorable and glorious riches, strengthen Your people. Fill their souls with the power of Your Spirit so that through faith the Anointed One will reside in their hearts. EPHESIANS 3:16-17 THE VOICE

What would it look like for Jesus to
take back what belongs to Him—the space in your
heart where He longs to dwell fully?

7. Declare & Believe

If you openly declare that Jesus is Lord and believe in your heart that God raised him from the dead, you will be saved. For it is by believing in your heart that you are made right with God, and it is by openly declaring your faith that you are saved. ROMANS 10:9-10 NLT

_Our goodness will never get us into heaven because
God's economy doesn't work that way._

8. To Be Holy

They were calling to one another: "Holy, holy, holy is
the Lord Almighty; the whole earth is full of his glory."
Isaiah 6:3 NIV

Our Holy God extends to us His holiness
through faith in the Holy One. Jesus Christ.

9. Let the Message Dwell

Let the message of Christ dwell among you richly as you teach and admonish one another with all wisdom through psalms, hymns, and songs from the Spirit, singing to God with gratitude in your hearts. COLOSSIANS 3:16 NIV

We're not meant to do this faith walk alone.
We need "soul sisters" to lead us back to the heart of
God and His Word.

10. Soaring High

Those who trust in the Lord will find new strength. They will soar high on wings like eagles. They will run and not grow weary. They will walk and not faint. Isaiah 40:31 NLT

God is who He says He is, and He
will always remain true to His Word.

11. Perfect and True

God's way is perfect. All the Lord's promises prove true.
He is a shield for all who look to him for protection. PSALM
18:30 NLT

When our lives are sewn together in real life, we get access to the backstory, present story, and redeemed story—and we see evidence of God's faithfulness and provision.

12. The Promised Helper

I will ask the Father to send you another Helper, the Spirit of truth, who will remain constantly with you. JOHN 14:16
THE VOICE

The most profound, life-changing principles in Scripture are often the hardest ones to understand.

13. A Quiet Life

Make it your goal to live a quiet life, minding your own business and working with your hands, just as we instructed you before. 1 THESSALONIANS 4:11 NLT

God has work for our hands to do.
The question is whether we will join Him in it.

14. Unity in Community

May the God who gives endurance and encouragement give you the same attitude of mind toward each other that Christ Jesus had, so that with one mind and one voice you may glorify the God and Father of our Lord Jesus Christ.
ROMANS 15:5-6 NIV

_____

_____

_____

_____

_____

_____

_____

_____

_____

_____

_____

_____

_____

_____

_____

_____

_____

_____

_____

At the very point when we feel as if we can't do community any longer, we need to rely all the more on the Holy Spirit to manifest in us and through us, prompting us to take the next step forward.

15. From Triggered to Trapped

We demolish arguments and every pretension that sets itself up against the knowledge of God, and we take captive every thought to make it obedient to Christ. 2 CORINTHIANS 10:5 NIV

Our senses will always a reaction.
but in Christ we can choose a respons
that lines up with the truth.

16. Transformed Living

Don't copy the behavior and customs of this world, but let God transform you into a new person by changing the way you think. ROMANS 12:2 NIV

Our inherited beliefs form a pattern of thought that shapes
the way we live, unless we allow God to challenge our
thinking and thereby transform our living.

17. Both/And

Notice how God is both kind and severe. He is severe toward those who disobeyed, but kind to you if you continue to trust in his kindness. ROMANS 11:22 NLT

God's attributes may seem opposite in their nature.
when they are actually necessary for balance.

18. Be Still

Be still and know that I am God! PSALM 46:10 NLT

_____

_____

_____

_____

_____

_____

_____

_____

_____

_____

_____

_____

_____

_____

_____

_____

_____

_____

_____

_____

The way we embrace stillness before God will be entirely reflected in the way He uniquely made each one of us.

19. Compassionate and Merciful

The Lord is compassionate and merciful, slow to get angry
and filled with unfailing love. PSALM 103:8 NIV

God's mercy isn't linked to a measuring stick.
He's not some hot-tempered, irrational killjoy ready
to ruin our lives with unquenchable anger.

20. Stone to Flesh

I will give you a new heart and put a new spirit in you; I will remove from you your heart of stone and give you a heart of flesh. EZEKIEL 36:26 NIV

The Lord can turn our stony hearts into His dwelling place, transforming us with one healing truth at a time.

21. Freed by Truth

Jesus said to the people who believed in him, "You are truly my disciples if you remain faithful to my teachings. And you will know the truth, and the truth will set you free." JOHN 8:31-32 NLT

Freedom in Christ is a soul-deep, unshakable, unquenchable gift that manifests in every single breath drawn from believing the truth.

22. Root and Fruit

The seeds on the rocky soil represent those who hear the message and receive it with joy. But since they don't have deep roots, they believe for a while, then they fall away when they face temptation. LUKE 8:31 NLT

If we are fickle gardeners of our faith, lacking
the perseverance to nurture the soil of our hearts,
we'll not experience the spiritual growth we crave.

23. No Trouble

See to it that no one falls short of the grace of God and that no bitter root grows up to cause trouble and defile many.
HEBREWS 12:15 NIV

_We might endure for a season, but that doesn't
mean our spiritual root system is healthy._

24. Love is the Goal

Let love be your highest goal! 1 CORINTHIANS 14:1 NLT

Love ushers in the kind of peace our hearts crave.

25. Unchangeable

One day Jesus left the crowds to pray alone. Only his disciples were with him, and he asked them, "Who do people say I am?" "Well," they replied, "some say John the Baptist, some say Elijah, and others say you are one of the other ancient prophets risen from the dead." Then he asked them, "But who do you say I am?" Peter replied, "You are the Messiah sent from God! Luke 9:18-20 NLT

The gospel message doesn't change, regardless
of what we choose to believe.

26. Redeemed for Good

You intended to harm me, but God intended it all for good. He brought me to this position so I could save the lives of many people. GENESIS 50:20 NLT

We may not be privy to God's redemptive
work in our story, but that doesn't mean He's stopped
accomplishing His purposes for His glory.

27. Our Hope

Let your unfailing love surround us, Lord, for our hope is in you alone. PSALM 33:22 NLT

When we put our hope in God Himself, we are actually placing everything about our lives in the arms of His love.

28. Good Gifts

"If you sinful people know how to give good gifts to your children, how much more will your heavenly Father give the Holy Spirit to those who ask him." LUKE 11:13 NLT

The good gift is actually the best gift God
can give us—the fullness of His presence through
the indwelling Holy Spirit promised by Him
when we place our faith in Jesus Christ.

29. All In

You must love the Lord your God with all your heart, all your soul, all your mind, and all your strength.

MARK 12:30 NLT

To give God everything changes everything.

30. This Power

When Simon saw that the Spirit was given when the
apostles laid their hands on people, he offered them money
to buy this power. "Let me have this power, too," he ex-
claimed, "so that when I lay my hands on people, they will
receive the Holy Spirit!" Acts 8:18-19 NLT

What a slippery slope we can easily fall onto when we
try to buy what God intended as a gift.

31. Owning Up

If we go around bragging, "We have no sin," then we are fooling ourselves and are strangers to the truth. But if we own up to our sins, God shows that He is faithful and just by forgiving us of our sins and purifying us from the pollution of all the bad things we have done. 1 John 1:8-9 The Voice

Without confession, sin becomes the stronghold that
insidiously infects every area of our lives.

32. Brand New

Anyone who belongs to Christ has become a new person. The old life is gone; a new life has begun! 2 CORINTHIANS 5:17 NLT

God takes us in any state and re-creates
our lives with glorious purpose.

33. Love Summed Up

The commandments say, "You must not commit adultery. You must not murder. You must not steal. You must not covet." These—and other such commandments—are summed up in this one commandment: "Love your neighbor as yourself. ROMANS 13:9 NLT

_____

_____

_____

_____

_____

_____

_____

_____

_____

_____

_____

_____

_____

_____

_____

_____

Loving our neighbors as ourselves requires
a kind of love in action that goes beyond the heart
and moves right into our hands and feet
homes and workplaces. every single day.

34. Even If

Even if that person wrongs you seven times a day and each time turns again and asks forgiveness, you must forgive.

Luke 17:4 NLT

Unforgiveness is like a cancer
on a mission to destroy our lives.

35. Sinner Saved

We are made right with God by placing our faith in Jesus Christ. And this is true for everyone who believes, no matter who we are. For everyone has sinned; we all fall short of God's glorious standard. ROMANS 3:22-23 NLT

_____

_____

_____

_____

_____

_____

_____

_____

_____

_____

_____

_____

_____

_____

_____

_____

_____

_____

_____

_____

_____

_____

Sin is woven deep into our stories, but
God's grace unravels its grip.

36. Pour Out Your Heart

O my people, trust in him at all times. Pour out your heart to him, for God is our refuge. PSALM 62:8 NLT

_____

_____

_____

_____

_____

_____

_____

_____

_____

_____

_____

_____

_____

_____

_____

_____

_____

_____

_____

_____

_____

*God is the One who most perfectly guards our hearts
as He provides safe refuge for our souls.*

37. Generous Grace

He gives grace generously. As the Scriptures say, "God opposes the proud but gives grace to the humble." JAMES 4:6 NLT

Through Jesus Christ, we receive the power
and presence of the Holy Spirit, who is always at work
in us, guiding us in what is good, right, and pure.

38. Gathering Together

Let us not neglect our meeting together, as some people do,
but encourage one another, especially now that the day of
his return is drawing near. HEBREWS 10:25 NLT

_____

_____

_____

_____

_____

_____

_____

_____

_____

_____

_____

_____

_____

_____

_____

_____

_____

_____

*Simply by gathering together, we become
an encouragement to each other.*

39. Wait Patiently

Wait patiently for the Lord. Be brave and courageous. Yes, wait patiently for the Lord. PSALM 27:4 NLT

While a season of waiting may feel purposeless, it's likely that God is using it to prepare us for what is yet to come.

40. Preparing to Endure

Prepare your minds for action and exercise self-control. Put all your hope in the gracious salvation that will come to you when Jesus Christ is revealed to the world. 1 PETER 1:13 NLT

In our world of instant gratification, exercising
self-control is a necessity for building spiritual endurance.

41. Quick. Slow. Slow.

Understand this, my dear brothers and sisters: You must all be quick to listen, slow to speak, and slow to get angry.
JAMES 1:19 NLT

_Have you ever considered the steps the
God of the Universe choreographed
for us to make our relationships thrive?_

42. Awesome and Impartial

For the Lord your God is God of gods and Lord of lords, the great, the mighty, and the awesome God, who is not partial and takes no bribe. DEUTERONOMY 10:17 ESV

God can't love you any more or less than
He already does today.

43. The Potter's Hands

What sorrow awaits those who argue with their Creator.
Does a clay pot argue with its maker? Does the clay dispute
with the one who shapes it, saying, "Stop, you're doing it
wrong!" Does the pot exclaim, "How clumsy can you be?"
Isaiah 45:9 NLT

Imagine how the Master Potter treasures us,
His masterpieces, because He's skillfully and
purposefully shaped us into His vessels.

44. Truth in Love

We will speak the truth in love, growing in every way more and more like Christ, who is the head of his body, the church. EPHESIANS 4:15 NLT

When the grace of God works its way
through our hearts first, His unchanging truth
can be fully delivered with love.

45. Holy Purpose

It will be your mission to open their eyes so that they may turn from darkness to light and from the kingdom of Satan to the kingdom of God. This is so that they may receive forgiveness of all their sins and have a place among those who are set apart for a holy purpose through having faith in Me.
ACTS 26:18 THE VOICE

The Light is for us, because Christ is for life.

46. The Thief is Real

The thief comes only to steal and kill and destroy. JOHN 10:10 NIV

Make no mistake. Satan is always busy at work.

47. Better Quantity and Quality

I have come that they may life, and have it to the full. JOHN 10:10 NIV

The life Jesus offers us is of better quantity and quality
than we'll find in anyone or anything else.

48. The Distress Cry

In my distress I cried out to the Lord; yes, I cried to my God for help. He heard me from his sanctuary; my cry reached his ears. 2 SAMUEL 22:7 NLT

How often we run from God when the
very thing we ought to do is cry out to Him
in our distress, even if we made the mess.

49. Anything and Everything

Don't worry about anything; instead, pray about everything. Tell God what you need, and thank him for all he has done. Then you will experience God's peace, which exceeds anything we can understand. His peace will guard your hearts and minds as you live in Christ Jesus.

PHILIPPIANS 4:6-7 NLT

When we give God our worry,
He gives us peace in return!

50. Put on Your New Self

You are ready to put on your new self, modeled after the very likeness of God: truthful, righteous, and holy.
EPHESIANS 4:24 THE VOICE

God will accomplish His work in us, but He requires
our wholehearted cooperation and participation!

51. What Time I Am Afraid

What time I am afraid, I will trust in thee. PSALM 56:3 KJV

Trusting in the Lord isn't about changing
the outcome. It's about learning to trust God
with the outcome, no matter what.

52. Secret Purpose

In him we were also chosen, having been predestined according to the plan of him who works out everything in conformity with the purpose of his will, in order that we, who were the first to put our hope in Christ, might be for the praise of his glory. EPHESIANS 1:11-12 NIV

His purposes are about what He's accomplishing in us
and through us rather than what He's doing with us.

53. Constant Conversation

Pray continually. 1 Thessalonians 5:17 niv

Prayer isn't one-sided! It's a two-way
conversation with God.

54. You Are More Valuable

What is the price of two sparrows—one copper coin? But not a single sparrow can fall to the ground without your Father knowing it. And the very hairs on your head are all numbered. So don't be afraid; you are more valuable to God than a whole flock of sparrows.

MATTHEW 10:29-31 NIV

Nothing God created is beyond His continual
and attentive sovereign care.

55. Sufficiently Full

My God will liberally supply (fill until full) your every need according to His riches in glory in Christ Jesus. PHILIPPIANS 4:19 AMP

It's time we gather around our tables. circle
up as families. and tell next generation about
what great things God has for us.

56. Approved by God

We speak as messengers approved by God to be entrusted with the Good News. Our purpose is to please God, not people. He alone examines the motives of our hearts.

1 THESSALONIANS 2:4 NLT

_____

_____

_____

_____

_____

_____

_____

_____

_____

_____

_____

_____

_____

_____

_____

_____

_____

*The temptation to please people becomes
an obstacle in sharing the gospel.*

57. This Is Real Love

This is real love—not that we loved God, but that he loved us and sent his Son as a sacrifice to take away our sins. Dear friends, since God loved us that much, we surely ought to love each other. 1 JOHN 4:10-11 NLT

The kind of love that comes from God isn't self-serving
or consuming—it is completely and utterly sacrificial.

58. Inner Soul Strength

I pray that from his glorious, unlimited resources he will empower you with inner strength through his Spirit.

EPHESIANS 3:16 NLT

We need soul strength, as in the kind of power
that comes from the glorious, unlimited resources of God
through the working of the Holy Spirit.

59. Story Hearts

Clearly, you are a letter from Christ showing the result of our ministry among you. This "letter" is written not with pen and ink, but with the Spirit of the living God. It is carved not on tablets of stone, but on human hearts.
2 CORINTHIANS 3:3 NLT

When God is about the business of writing a
story on our hearts, He'll use life and death, blessings
and trials, for His glory and kingdom purposes.

60. For Such a Time

And who knows but that you have come to your royal position for such a time as this? ESTHER 4:14 NIV

We are divinely appointed by God to take up our
"royal position" as servants of King Jesus "for such a time
as this" in the great rescue of His lost children.

61. Do Not Fear

Do not fear, for I am with you; do not be dismayed, for I am your God. I will strengthen you and help you; I will uphold you with my righteous right hand. ISAIAH 41:10 NIV

Overcoming fear isn't about thinking less
about the things that make us afraid.
It's about thinking more upon the promises of God, who
declares there is no need to live in fear.

62. Heart-Centered Hospitality

Offer hospitality to one another without grumbling.

1 Peter 4:9 niv

Heart-centered hospitality requires making
people more important than things and remembering that
relationships matter more than the setting.

63. Beckoning Onward

I'm not saying that I have this all together, that I have it made. But I am well on my way, reaching out for Christ, who has so wondrously reached out for me. Friends, don't get me wrong: By no means do I count myself an expert in all of this, but I've got my eye on the goal, where God is beckoning us onward—to Jesus. I'm off and running, and I'm not turning back. PHILIPPIANS 3:12-14 MSG

_In this spiritual journey, it's the long race we need to
condition ourselves for as we keep pressing on._

64. The Blessing of Submission

Submit to one another out of reverence for Christ.

EPHESIANS 5:21 NIV

If we are willing to embrace the call to biblical
submission. we'll uncover the most precious gifts
hidden in the very places God hems us in.

65. Chosen and Called

You are a chosen people. You are royal priests, a holy nation, God's very own possession. As a result, you can show others the goodness of God, for he called you out of the darkness into his wonderful light. 1 PETER 2:9 NLT

When we believe we are chosen as God's very own
possession, everything about our life's purpose changes.

66. Enter into Rest

There is a special rest still waiting for the people of
God. For all who have entered into God's rest have rested
from their labors, just as God did after creating the world.
HEBREWS 4:9-10 NLT

_____

_____

_____

_____

_____

_____

_____

_____

_____

_____

_____

_____

_____

_____

_____

_____

_____

_____

_____

_____

_____

_____

*God invites and commands us to enter into rest,
but it's up to us to submit and receive this gift.*

67. Never Failing

The word of God will never fail. LUKE 1:37 NLT

The Word of God is true always
because God is always true.

68. Your True Treasure

Wherever your treasure is, there the desires of your heart will also be. MATTHEW 6:21 NLT

We are not the ones who go about saving souls,
but we are Christ's ambassadors commissioned to be
His hands and feet and mouthpieces on this earth.

69. Blessed Is the One

Blessed is the one who does not walk in step with the wicked or stand in the way that sinners take or sit in the company of mockers, but whose delight is in the law of the Lord, and who meditates on his law day and night. That person is like a tree planted by streams of water, which yields its fruit in season and whose leaf does not wither—whatever they do prospers. PSALM 1:1-3 NIV

Whether we're walking, standing, sitting, sleeping,
or daydreaming, the Word is to be on our mind.

70. Give Your Burdens

Give your burdens to the Lord, and he will take care of
you. He will not permit the godly to slip and fall. PSALM
55:22 NLT

How often do we insist on carrying an emotional
and spiritual burden that is greater than what we can
humanly handle, all while Jesus stands before us
and offers to carry it for us?

71. Cast Your Cares

Cast all your anxiety on him because he cares for you.
1 Peter 5:7 nlt

If God acknowledges how our cares can consume
us, then shouldn't we turn them over to Him?

72. Suffering Our Share

We are pressed on every side by troubles, but we are not crushed. We are perplexed, but not driven to despair. We are hunted down, but never abandoned by God. We get knocked down, but we are not destroyed. Through suffering, our bodies continue to share in the death of Jesus so that the life of Jesus may also be seen in our bodies.

2 Corinthians 4:8-11 nlt

We don't have to face suffering with a defeated mind-set
when we remember our victory is found in the cross.

73. Build Each Other Up

Encourage each other and build each other up, just as you are already doing. 1 THESSALONIANS 5:11 NLT

God designed us to be His hands and feet as we seek authentic ways to encourage one another and build each other up in word and deed, by example and by faith.

74. Kindness and Grace

He is so rich in kindness and grace that he purchased our
freedom with the blood of his Son and forgave our sins.

EPHESIANS 1:7 NLT

God is so kind. He poured out
His grace for our freedom.

75. When We Ask

Keep on asking, and you will receive what you ask for. Keep on seeking, and you will find. Keep on knocking, and the door will be opened to you. For everyone who asks, receives. Everyone who seeks, finds. And to everyone who knocks, the door will be opened. MATTHEW 7:7-8 NLT

When God invites us to ask Him for everything and
anything. He doesn't turn a blind eye to the state of our
hearts and His kingdom purposes.

76. No Regrets

The kind of sorrow God wants us to experience leads us away from sin and results in salvation. There's no regret for that kind of sorrow. But worldly sorrow, which lacks repentance, results in spiritual death. 2 CORINTHIANS 7:10 NLT

Through our honest confession of sin before God,
we find the freedom from guilt our souls crave.

77. Ministry of Generosity

As a result of your ministry, they will give glory to God. For your generosity to them and to all believers will prove that you are obedient to the Good News of Christ.

2 Corinthians 9:13 nlt

We have the freedom in Christ to decide how we'll sow into kingdom work—will it be generously or reluctantly?

78. For the Good

We know that God causes everything to work together for the good of those who love God and are called according to his purpose for them. ROMANS 8:28 NLT

Yes it is true—God works for the good of those
who love Him, always and in all situations.

79. The Same But Different

There are different kinds of spiritual gifts, but the same
Spirit is the source of them all. There are different kinds of
service, but we serve the same Lord. God works in different
ways, but it is the same God who does the work in all of us.
1 Corinthians 12:4-6 NLT

_____

_____

_____

_____

_____

_____

_____

_____

_____

_____

_____

_____

_____

_____

_____

_____

_____

Yes. God created within us a gift to be used for the greater good in the body of Christ.

80. Everyday Missionary

By God's grace and mighty power, I have been given the
privilege of serving him by spreading this Good News.
EPHESIANS 3:7 NLT

We can be everyday missionaries in the
most unlikely of mission fields.

81. Steady that Mind

You will keep in perfect peace those whose minds are steadfast, because they trust in you. ISAIAH 6:3 NLT

If we don't steady our minds on God's truth,
we can fret ourselves into a hot mess.

82. Worthy Already

We keep on praying for you, asking our God to enable you to live a life worthy of his call. May he give you the power to accomplish all the good things your faith prompts you to do. 1 THESSALONIANS 1:11 NLT

Our worth is secure in Christ, and our
purpose is defined by God alone.

83. Serving the Creator

They traded the truth about God for a lie. So they worshiped and served the things God created instead of the Creator himself, who is worthy of eternal praise! Amen.
ROMANS 1:25 NLT

We need to learn how to live in the "undone" of life,
because our "doings" are not greater than the One who
made us to accomplish all things for His glory.

84. Refreshment Redefined

The generous will prosper; those who refresh others will themselves be refreshed. PROVERBS 11:25 NLT

Maybe we need to let go of what we do have
to receive the "more" God has in store for us.

85. Let It Flow

Anyone who believes in me may come and drink! For the Scriptures declare, "Rivers of living water will flow from his heart." JOHN 7:38 NLT

What would we bring to this world if we were so filled up with Jesus that all that ever flowed out of us was more of Him!

86. Kept and Recorded

You keep track of all my sorrows. You have collected all my tears in your bottle. You have recorded each one in your book. PSALM 56:8 NLT

Our mere human souls can't handle all the sorrows
and tears that come our way, but God can.

87. Proven Promises

God's way is perfect. All the Lord's promises prove true.
He is a shield for all who look to him for protection.

2 Samuel 22:31 NLT

_Our doubting of God's ways doesn't
ever change His promises._

88. Tell Them

The dead cannot praise you; they cannot raise their voices in praise. Those who go down to the grave can no longer hope in your faithfulness. Only the living can praise you as I do today. Each generation tells of your faithfulness to the next.
ISAIAH 38:18-19 NLT

When we personally encounter God's faithfulness
and forgiveness, healing and holiness, love and redemption,
grace and mercy, we can't help but praise Him.

89. Shine On

Let your light shine everywhere you go, that you may il-
lumine creation, so men and women everywhere may see
your good actions, may see creation at its fullest, may see
your devotion to Me, and may turn and praise your Father
in heaven because of it. Matthew 5:15-16 THE VOICE

We are His disciples. His ambassadors.
His children. We are "brand" Jesus.

90. May God Be With You

Dear brothers and sisters, I close my letter with these last words: Be joyful. Grow to maturity. Encourage each other. Live in harmony and peace. Then the God of love and peace will be with you. May the grace of the Lord Jesus Christ, the love of God, and the fellowship of the Holy Spirit be with you all. 2 CORINTHIANS 13:11,14

God doesn't waste a second in our lives.
He uses even our passing connections in
His sanctifying and transforming work.

Let's Continue Together

It is a blessing to be able to inspire and equip you to embrace a fresh encounter with God and His Word.

I hope you will reach out to me and let me know how this experience has deepened your faith.

Join me at MoretoBe.com and feel free to reach out to me by email at elisa@moretobe.com.

I'm here cheering you on and praying for you.

MORETOBE.COM

Made in the USA
Middletown, DE
06 March 2019